*The Ceremony of Initiation:
Analysis & Commentary*

By W. L. Wilmshurst

Copyright © 2020 Lamp of Trismegistus. All rights reserved. No part of this publication may be reproduced or transmitted in any form or by any means, electronic or mechanical, including photocopying, recording, or by any information storage and retrieval system, without permission in writing from Lamp of Trismegistus. Reviewers may quote brief passages.

ISBN: 978-1-63118-473-4

*Foundations of Freemasonry
Series*

Other Books in this Series and Related Titles

Masonic and Rosicrucian History by M P Hall & H Voorhis (978-1-63118-486-4)

The Influence of Pythagoras on Freemasonry and Other Essays (978-1-63118-404-8)

Freemasonry, Mithraism and the Ancient Mysteries by various (978-1-63118-407-9)

The Master Mason's Handbook by J S M Ward (978-1-63118-474-1)

The Kabbalah of Masonry & Related Writings by E Levi &c (978-1-63118-453-6)

Some Deeper Aspects of Masonic Symbolism by A E Waite (978-1-63118-461-1)

Masonic Symbolism of King Solomon's Temple by A Mackey &c (978-1-63118-442-0)

The Old Past Master by Carl H Claudy (978-1-63118-464-2)

The Mysteries of Freemasonry & the Druids by various (978-1-63118-444-4)

Rosicrucians and Speculative Masonry in the Seventeenth Century (978-1-63118-489-5)

The Two Great Pillars of Boaz and Jachin by A Mackey &c (978-1-63118-433-8)

The Regius Poem or Halliwell Manuscript by King Solomon (978-1-63118-447-5)

The Lost Keys of Freemasonry or The Secret of Hiram Abiff (978-1-63118-427-7)

Masonic Symbolism of the Apron & the Altar by various (978-1-63118-428-4)

Symbolism and Discourses on the Entered Apprentice, Fellowcraft and Master Mason Blue Lodge Degrees by various (978-1-63118-413-0)

The Legend of the Holy Grail and its Connection with Templars and Freemasons by A E Waite (978-1-63118-462-8)

American Indian Freemasonry by A C Parker (978-1-63118-460-4)

Ancient Mysteries and Secret Societies by M P Hall (978-1-63118-410-9)

The Janeites, The Man Who Would Be King and Other Stories of Freemasonry by Rudyard Kipling (978-1-63118-480-2)

Audio Versions are also available on Audible, Amazon and Apple

Table of Contents

Series Introduction...7

The Ceremony of Initiation
Introduction...9

Part I
The Admission...21
The Prayer of Dedication...23
The Perambulation or Mystical Journeying...25
The Professions of Freedom, Motive, and Perseverance...29
The Advance from West to East...31
The Obligation...33
The Restoration to Light...37
Summary of Part I...41

Part II
The Revelation of the Greater and the Lesser Lights...43
The Entrustment with the Secrets...51
The Testing by the Wardens...57
The Investiture with the Apron...61
The Charge in the N.E. Corner...65
The Working Tools...71
The Tracing Board...75
Conclusion...79
A Note upon the Frontispiece...83

INTRODUCTION

From the beginning of Modern Freemasonry's birthdate of 1717, the intelligentsia of humanity have found refuge for safe reflection within the walls of the fraternity. Masonic writers have produced a nearly incalculable amount of written musings on a multitude of esoteric and philosophical subjects, as they relate to the ancient mysteries that Freemasonry currently storehouses. Sadly, most of it appears to have sat largely unread, as American Freemasonry in particular, continues to transform itself into something that bears little resemblance to what it was originally designed to be. The true essence of Freemasonry is not that of blind patriotism or a single-minded national religion but one of Universal Brotherhood and altruism, designed for the betterment not just of its members but of society as a whole. In particular, for those who are not members of the fraternity, as Freemasonry has always acted as a beacon, to help guide humanity through darker times, with the hopes that one day we will collectively reach a truly enlightened age.

It's not uncommon for new members joining the fraternity to find little education within the walls of many modern lodges, in spite of so much written material available to the membership. Many older members are not simply uneducated with regards to real Masonic history and symbology, not to mention the vast arena of related subjects, but they are disinterested in all of it, as well.

Lamp of Trismegistus is doing its part to help preserve humanity's Masonic history by making some of these classics available to those students who are seeking to unearth the knowledge of these ancient colossi. As such, Lamp of Trismegistus offers its readers highlights of Masonic study, culled from a variety of authors and viewpoints, with the hope bringing education back into the fraternity. So, be sure to check out other titles in our *Foundations of Freemasonry Series* as well as our *Theosophical Classics, Occult Fiction, Paranormal Research Series, Esoteric Classics, Supernatural Fiction, Studies in Buddhism* and our *Christian Apocrypha Series* as well as numerous other subjects; and, don't be afraid to let a little altruism into your own heart or even into your Lodge. You can also download the audio versions of many of these titles from Apple, Amazon or Audible, for learning on the go.

The Ceremony of Initiation

INTRODUCTION

I

These notes are intended as a Manual of Instruction for the benefit of Masons who have recently taken their First Degree, and for that of other Brethren wishful to understand the purpose and the meaning of the Initiation Ceremony. The endeavor to indicate the reason for the existence of the Masonic system, to draw aside the veil of allegory and symbolism in which the Initiation Ceremony is clothed, and to reveal its spirit and subsurface significance.

The First Degree Ceremony used on the reception of a Candidate into the Craft is designed to introduce him to the first stage of a system of knowledge and self-discipline which, if faithfully followed up and lived out in his personal life, will clarify and transform his mind from its natural state of darkness to one of Light, i.e., expanded clear-seeing spiritual consciousness raised far beyond and existing independently of the perceptions of the natural senses. It is, therefore called a Ceremony of Initiation from *in ire* to go inwards, i.e., beyond the merely material surfaces of things), and because it is meant to mark the beginning (initium) of a new order of personal life and consciousness. It might equally well be called one of Regeneration or Rebirth; indeed its parallel in Religion is the sacrament of Baptism, which is the initial incident of the religious life and is performed at the West end of a Church, just as a Masonic Candidate enters the Lodge and begins his

Masonic career in the symbolic West. It is a ceremony provided to give an answer to what the Candidate professes to be the predominant wish of his heart – a wish well expressed by probably the oldest prayer in the world, which is still used daily by millions of our fellowmen in the East:—

From the unreal lead me to the Real; From the darkness lead me to Light; From the mortal bring me to Immortality!

The presence or absence of this aspiration in a Candidate should be the test of his fitness for Initiation. Any less exalted motive for seeking Initiation falls short of the true intention. The Candidate's attitude should be one of definite intelligent expectation of spiritual good to come to him, and of positive aspiration and heart-hunger for it; equally definitely it must not be for any material or social advantage, nor a merely negative state of curiosity or uncertainty as to what is to be found in the Craft.

II

For every Candidate the Initiation Ceremony implies that whatever academic or scientific learning he possesses, whatever philosophical ideas he holds, whatever religious creed he professes, prior to Initiation, there remains something more – indeed something vastly more – for him yet to learn and to which the Craft can help to lead him. This does not mean that he will necessarily discover his previous convictions to be false; on the other hand, so far as they be true he will find abundant confirmation and amplification of them, and so far as they are erroneous or imperfect he will learn to modify them. It means that he must be prepared to find some of his wonted and perhaps even most deeply rooted ideas to be apprehensions of Truth so partial and limited that they operate as obstructions to the wider vision which might be his, and that the more tenaciously he clings to them the more he may be blocking his own light. If, therefore, he is to profit by the Light to which the Craft leads he must be prepared to keep his mind open and fluid and to make such mental self-surrender as occasion warrants. We all tend to feel so certain of ourselves, so wise in our own conceits, and too often are unaware that we have much to unlearn before we can become truly teachable. But from earliest times the Candidate for Initiation has been called a "child" and taught to regard himself as such.

Accordingly the divesting of the Candidate's person prior to the Ceremony is symbolic of the mental unclothing required of him, whilst his self-abandonment to be taken wherever he is led and to do whatever he is told betokens the meekness and docility with which his mind should follow Truth wherever it may lead. even into apparently perilous places and among ideas not recognized by the conventions and orthodoxies of the world without. For true Initiation involves a spiritual adventure, a voyage of the mind, not into the unknowable but into what the Candidate has never yet known or experienced; and it leads to regions where he travels farthest who carries least burdens, where he acquires most who casts away most of himself, and where the really heart-hungry are increasingly filled with good things from which the intellectually rigid and the rich in conventional knowledge are automatically precluded. To the single-minded. Wisdom has ways of revealing itself which the learned understand not.

Mental self-tripping and readjustment is, of course, not a sudden, but a gradual process. No Candidate is called upon to do undue or too sudden violence to himself, but rather to adapt himself gradually to the new conditions and to become transformed by a slow but steady renewing of his mind and outlook. See how this is evidenced by his progressive unclothing as he passes on from Degree to Degree! In the First only certain parts of his person are bared; in the Second, only certain other and complementary parts. It is not until the Third Degree that the maximum unclothing is called for, by that time he is presumed to be inured to self-surrender and better able to make the larger sacrifice which that sublime Degree involves.

III

To turn now to the Ceremony itself. Up to about the year 1700, formally compiled Rituals did not exist. The working was transmitted orally. There was no such thing as a memorized form mechanically repeated with such word-perfectness and dignified elocution as may be, but an extempore pronouncement of real power and spiritual efficacy, performed by a Master possessing complete understanding of what he did, and able to adapt or amplify the ceremony in accordance with the culture, intelligence and probable requirements of a properly prepared Candidate. The actual form of words employed was (and still always is) the least important element about the Ceremony. What is of far vaster consequence is the ability of the Initiator, and those co-operating with him, to infuse into such spiritual fervor and emotional momentum that what is done and said over the Candidate shall penetrate his heart and mind, and awaken certain truths in his soul, – a result requiring, as its first condition, that the Candidate be a fit and proper person and properly prepared for it.

Even today, the Irish and many Continental Masonic Constitutions work to no set ritual. Certain traditional landmarks and age-old usages are uniformly observed, but for the rest (e.g. The various charges, explanations, and entrustings) the wording of the Ceremony is left to the inspiration and emotion of the moment.

The Ritual which, with slight local variations, has become traditional with us, embodies all these land-marks and usages, and has been compiled with extraordinary and, indeed, inspired skill and wisdom. To treat it superficially, or regard it as a composition to be reeled off one's memory in a "non-stop" fashion, is to miss the purport and the beauties of a highly complex and comprehensive compilation. Analysis of it shows that it is built up of fourteen distinct "movements" or episodes, in two series of seven each.

The first series is associated with the Candidate's state of darkness; it is an ascending or crescendo series rising, like an emotional wave, to a climax at the moment of his symbolic restoration to Light. The second series is associated with the state of Light to which he has been lifted up; it is a descending or diminuendo series dealing with matters consequent upon his attainment of Light; the emotional billow, as it were, dies gradually away, but leaving the Candidate's being flooded with new perceptions and stimulated by a quickening influence such as he never previously knew and which will probably take him some time to assimilate.

The sequence of these episodes is as follows; and they will indicate what a large range of ideas has been compressed within a short Ceremony :—

STATE OF DARKNESS.

1. The Admission to the Lodge.

2. The Prayer of Dedication.

3. The Mystical Journey (or Perambulation).

4. The Declarations of Freedom, Motive, and Perseverance.

5. The Advance from W. to E.

6. The Obligation.

7. The Restoration to Light.

STATE OF LIGHT.

8. The Revelation of the Greater and Lesser Lights.

9. The Entrustment with the Secrets.

10. The Testing by the Wardens.

11. The Investiture with the Clothing.

12. The Instruction in the N.E.

13. The Instruction in the Working Tools.

14. The Instruction in the Tracing Board.

Each of these fourteen incidents provides scope for prolonged reflection and comment, but in these notes only brief observations can be made upon each of them in succession.

The separation of the Ceremony into two main sub-divisions, the "state of Darkness" and the "state of Light," has a far-reaching allusiveness; first to cosmic truth and in relation to human life generally; secondly, historically and in correspondence with the Ancient Mysteries.

Cosmically, all human life begins its quest for Light and Truth in a state of darkness as our nature, our purpose and destiny. We are, as it were, born blind or hoodwinked about them; as the Ancients taught, we have all drunk the cup of Lethe and the water of forgetfulness before descending to birth in the flesh. Our quest, therefore, at the outset of our earthly career must necessarily be a darkened one, a mere hoodwinked fumbling about for we know not what, until the pains, sorrows, and disillusionments of existence awake us to the fact that we are wasting our substance among shadows and futilities, and that there may be something higher and better worth hunting for. This preliminary condition of mind and soul the Initiates likened to being in a place which they called "the Hall of Ignorance" or "the Hall of Truth in Darkness," in which we grope about for a Light and Wisdom which are at all times around us, but which we cannot find because our faculties are as yet sealed from perceiving them.

Later on, when experience has caused a man to turn away in distaste from outer interests to the quest of better things, he becomes initiated in to the science of them, and was said to have entered the "Hall of Learning" or the "Hall of Truth in Light," for by this time he is no longer ignorantly groping in the dark, but has become actuated by a definite and enlightened resolve to find the Reality behind the shadows.

It is these two conditions, one of groping ignorantly and with blinded eyes for the Reality behind temporal existence, and one of seeking it intelligently and with the opened eyes of the Initiate, that are reproduced in the two subdivisions of our First Degree Ceremony. There remains a third condition, but for the novice it is as yet a long way off and is, therefore, beyond the purview of our present enquiry; its attainment is described as entering the "Hall of Wisdom," which is possible only to Master Masons who have passed beyond the two previous "Halls," and whose search has been rewarded with finding the ultimate secrets of life.

Preceding the actual Ceremony, however, there is implied a preliminary and very necessary routine, – the due Preparation of the Candidate, some remarks upon which must preface our commentary upon the fourteen points of the Ceremony itself

As to the sources of the Ceremony, it (as also the official E.A. Lecture and Tracing Board Explanation provided to interpret it) is a blend of various streams of influence. The chief of these is the traditional method – usually called the "Secret Doctrine" – common to all the Ancient Mysteries and Initiation systems from the dawn of history; a method and doctrine always held in reserve from the knowledge of the masses of the people, constituting stronger "meat" and imparting deeper truths than the more simple instruction, or "milk," provided for the general public by the current education and religious institutions of a given time or place. As is well known to students of the history of religion, behind the exoteric doctrine of every great Teacher or religious Founder, has always existed an esoteric counterpart of it for advanced disciples.

Combined with elements of this ancient esoteric wisdom are elements from more recent cognate systems, such as Hermeticism, the Hebrew Cabala, and Rosicrucianism, as also survivals from mediaeval Gild Masonry, whilst the Holy Scriptures which have served to nourish the religious life of the West are interfused with all these and act as a unifying and explanatory "great light."

Accordingly we find our Masonic Ritual, as the offspring of these sources, continually using the language of its parents, speaking now in the terms or symbols of one and now in those of another of them; and it becomes clear that all these sources have been stewards of the same Mysteries, that they proclaim the same truth and mean the same thing, and can be constantly cross-referenced and found to be mutually interpretative.

Take one of a host of possible examples – the Preparation of the Candidate. The Craft requires every Candidate for Initiation to come "properly prepared." In Religion this paralleled by the Church requiring its neophytes to be "prepared" for Confirmation into fuller realization of spiritual life. And every ancient and modern Initiation system has required it; indeed the preparation insisted on an antiquity and in more advanced secret Orders than the Craft, was, and still is, of an extremely intensive character. But the point to be stressed here is that, for those who really desire Light, a preliminary orientation of will, heart and mind is indispensable to their desire becoming fulfilled, and "Prepare ye the way of the Lord!" is the Biblical confirmation of what the Ancient Mysteries required and what the Craft still inculcates. And when, with us, the Master of the Lodge dispatches his Deacon to prepare the Candidate for his reception, is he not still echoing and giving a personal value to words of impersonal and cosmic application. "Behold, I will send my messenger to prepare the way before me"?

IV

The mental preparation of the Candidate should have been proceeding for a considerable time before the Ceremony is conferred. It can be considerably assisted by his Masonic sponsors upon whom rests the responsibility of vouching for his fitness for Initiation, and who in private converse can adumbrate to him a broad idea of what is involved, and assure themselves of his sympathetic response to it.

As to the symbolic preparation of his external person, much closer attention is paid to this in Continental Lodges than is usual with us. He is taken to a quiet ante-room and there left alone for some time to compose his mind and read some sentences warning him of the solemnity of his project and the desirability of proceeding with it in a spirit of meekness and confidence or of withdrawing from it while there is yet time.

After an interval he is interviewed by the Deacon and asked for his decision. If he desires to proceed he is then asked to write brief replies to some such questions as these :—(1) What is your view of the purpose of human life and the nature of human destiny? (2) What is your object in seeking to be initiated? (3) What may the Craft hope to receive from you in return for what you expect to receive from it? He is left to write his replies, which are then taken into the Lodge and submitted to the Master's approval, who declares whether they are satisfactory, in which event only the ballot is taken. Upon his election the Deacon is dispatched to greet the Candidate with the tidings and to invite him to surrender his metals and money. After which the formal preparation of his person proceeds as with us; this being done with solemnity, the reason for each separate act of preparation being briefly explained by the Deacon.

It were well if the above practice or an approximation of it were always followed. In any event great importance attaches to the due performance of the Deacon's ministrations so as to create the most favorable mental conditions for the Candidate before he enter the Lodge. (The symbolic value of the Deacon's work is explained in our Lodge Paper No. 4, and it is in the spirit of that explanation that he should discharge his duties).

If it be essential that the Candidate should enter the Lodge properly prepared, it is equally important that those waiting to receive and initiate him should themselves be prepared in heart and intention to do so. Even the atmosphere of the Temple should be prepared by rendering it peaceful and free of commotion The W.M. can ensure this by enjoying complete silence during the interval preceding the Candidate's entrance and inviting the Brethren to reflect upon the nature of the work in hand and to unite with him in earnest aspiration that that work may be spiritually effectual.

The unofficiating Brethren present are not meant to be mere spectators of the Ceremony. The whole Lodge, and not only the acting officials of it, should participate in the mystery. Great is the power of united concentrated thought and intention in impressing a Candidate's mentality and awaking it to new and spiritual perceptions; and to this end the spoken work of the Master and Officers actively concerned can be very greatly assisted by the silent mental co-operation of the unofficiating Brethren.

PART I
1 – The Admission

From the place of preparation the Candidate is led to the door of the Lodge. This he finds close tyled. He "meets with opposition" (as the E.A. Lecture says) and cannot gain admission save in the prescribed way.

In other words, on turning from the world without to the world within, his first discovery is to find his way blocked by an intervening barrier. What is that barrier? What does the door of the Lodge symbolize?

Obviously it symbolizes some obstructive element in himself. He is made to recognize that any opposition to his own spiritual advancement comes from within himself and must be overcome by his own efforts. (Hence it is that the Candidate is required to give the knocks himself; they should never be given for him by anyone else.)

The purport of this episode is expressly declared in the E.A. Lecture to be subjective and mystical. The knocks are there stated to be interpretable in the light of the Scriptural direction, "Ask and ye shall have; Seek and ye shall find; Knock and it shall be opened to you." This threefold direction, observe, not only corresponds with the triple knocks, but also with the triple faculties of the Candidate himself. He should "ask" with the prayerful aspirations of his heart; he should "seek" with the intellectual activities of his mind; he should "knock" with the force of his bodily energies. He who hopes to find the Light within must devote his entire being to the quest; it demands and engages the attention of the whole man.

How true to life and to psychology is this symbolic opposition at the door of the Lodge! We all erect our mental barriers. The habitual thought-methods, prejudices, preconceptions and "fixed ideas" in which we indulge in the course of life in the outer world, become obstructions to the perception of things of the world within. They create mental deposits which condense and harden, until they obscure the wider, deeper, clearer vision we might have but for own self-created limitations. We erect and tyle our own door against ourselves and block our own light, and eventually on seeking to turn to the Light find ourselves confronted by darkness and opposition of our own creating. And it is just these barriers that must be broken down by our own efforts and the force of our own persistent "knocks."

For "knocks" it may be helpful to think of a more modern term, – vibrations. Persistent vibrations, in a given direction will, as is well known, eventually break down whatever is opposed to them, whether physical or mental. Vibrations of faith remove mountains. Vibrations of intellectual energy result in the solution of problems. Vibrations of emotion break through into the hearts of others. Vibration of spiritual aspiration penetrate into higher worlds and open doors into them. And all this is signified by the simple incident of the Candidate meeting with opposition at the door of the Lodge and gaining admission as the result of his own symbolic knocks.

2 – The Prayer of Dedication

The initial act of the Ceremony is appropriately a prayer by the assembled Brethren (1) that the Candidate (who has already been elected to formal membership of the Craft) may now become **spiritually** incorporated into the Great Brotherhood, and (2) for his endowment with such an influx of **wisdom** as, by virtue of that incorporation, will give him increasing **power** to manifest the **beauty** of holiness.

The brevity and simplicity of this prayer are liable to obscure its deep implications. Observe (from the three words just emboldened above) that it contains the first unobtrusive reference to that trinity of Wisdom, Strength and Beauty of which the Candidate will hear later on, and of which it is prayed that he may become a living manifestation.

Note too, that there is no reference in the prayer to morality of merely ethical virtues; it invokes something far loftier than these, – the gift of the Spirit; it strikes a keynote intended to govern the tone of both the Ceremony and the Candidate's whole after-life.

Observe, too, that it is not a prayer by the Candidate (who is required only to "kneel and listen" to it), but one for him and for the Craft itself; it is a prayer that the spiritual efficiency of the whole Fraternity may become augmented by this new accession to it. Every Brother present, therefore, should unite with the Chaplain in a strong tension of aspiration that the prayer may become realized in the joint interests of both the Craft and its new member. Later on, the latter should make the prayer his own, remembering throughout his life that it was once offered over him in his darkness and helplessness on behalf of the whole Craft, and that it falls to himself to justify increasingly the invocation then so solemnly made in his behalf.

3 – The Perambulation or Mystical Journeying

Next follows the Perambulation. But this preceded by an inquiry to the Candidate; where does he repose reliance in circumstances of danger and difficulty? It is obvious that he is about to be exposed to circumstances of that character, and the question is therefore put to ascertain whether he ought to be allowed to expose himself to them or not. The answer to the question should always be his own and should spring spontaneously from his own mind and lips; to prompt him with an answer detracts from the reality of the Ceremony and encourages him to give a reply which may be insincere. The Ceremony implies that if he cannot voluntarily give the proper response to the question, he is unfit for Initiation and should be led back out of the Lodge. If, on the other hand, he responds satisfactorily, well and good; the Ceremony may proceed and will be a test of the Candidate's profession of faith.

What are the dangers and difficulties he is about to be exposed to? In our Ceremony they are, of course, merely theoretic and symbolic. But in the Initiation Rites of the Ancient Mysteries (of which ours are a faint echo) they were extremely exacting, realistic and affrighting, and such as put a Candidate to severe tests of mental stability and moral fitness. They may be read about more fully in literature on the subject, from which it will be gathered how very essential it was that a Candidate for Initiation into the secrets and mysteries of his own being should possess not only a stable faith and moral center, but also a sound mind in a sound body. Otherwise grave responsibility rested upon both the Initiators and the

Candidate, and grave risks of damage to the latter's reason attached by suffering an unfit person to "rashly run forward" towards experiences for which he was unsuited.

Hence it is that a Candidate is still called upon to make a public declaration of faith and to be passed in review before the Lodge ere the Ceremony is proceeded with, so that his Initiators may be satisfied of his fitness.

This is the first reason for the ceremonial Perambulation. But there is another, of equal importance. The journey around the Lodge is a symbolic representation of the Candidate's own life-journeyings in this world prior to his request for Initiation into the world within. The dangers and difficulties referred to are the vicissitudes encountered in his own personal Odyssey; indeed the wanderings and buffetings of Odysseus are an ancient poetic allegory of these experiences, of a like character to the parable of the career of the Prodigal Son before he "came to himself" and struck the true path.

We must observe two most noteworthy details in connection with this symbolic journey. The first is that, though in a state of darkness himself, he is not alone, but has with him an enlightened guide. Moreover he is compassed about by a cloud of witnesses keenly anxious for his spiritual advancement and restoration to light. The significance of this detail is that every traveler through life has within himself his own invisible guide and that his soul's upward struggles are observed by many unseen watchers.

The second is that in the course of his symbolic journey he is led to each Warden in turn, whom, by a particular gesture, he as it were arouses from silence and stirs to utterance. The gesture itself is in fact a repetition of the knocks previously given at the door of the Lodge. But whereas those knocks were first addressed to inert material (the door), they are now applied to a living being (the Warden). What does this imply? It signifies that in our efforts to turn away from the outer world and penetrate to the Light of the inner one, we not only overcome our own self-created opposition, but we awaken and stimulate into activity certain living but hitherto dormant energies within ourselves.

Of those latent energies with him the Candidate will come to learn more later. Suffice it for the moment to know that his desire for Light awakens real but as yet slumbering potencies within himself, which from now onwards will become stimulated and promote his spiritual advancement. In each of us reside certain dormant principles (represented by the two Wardens) higher - than the normal benighted human reasons knows* [* These latent spiritual principles in man, symbolized by the Wardens or "Watchmen," are frequently referred to in the V.S.L., e.g. "I have set watchmen upon thy walls which shall never hold their peace day nor night" (Is. 62, 8); "Unless the Lord keep the city the watchman waketh but in vain," (Ps. 127, 1).]; it is these which it is possible to provoke into activity, and which, then awakened, no longer block our passage but speed a man on his ways with, as it were, the mystical greeting: "Pass, Good Report!"

The expression "Good Report" is a modern form of a very ancient mystical title accorded to the Candidate. It means much more than "good reputation" in the popular sense of the phrase. It implies that the Candidate's nature is one animated by spiritual sincerity, one that rings true like a coin, and that sounds forth a convincing note when it speaks. "True of voice" was the Egyptian form of "Good Report," and it is for this reason that, on approaching each Warden, our present Candidates are called upon to sound forth their own note so that the Warden may determine whether they are indeed "true of voice" and qualified to be passed on.

"Say something that I may see you" said Socrates to a shy youth who sought his instruction, for a man's speech betrays him to the sensitive ear, which is able to judge of the speaker's sincerity and spiritual status. And hence it is that the Candidate is required to sound forth his own voice to the Wardens.

4 – The Professions of Freedom, Motive, and Perseverance

After both Wardens have assured themselves of the Candidate's fitness for advancement to the East, he is so certified and presented to the Master for Initiation. But before the Master accepts him the Candidate is required to pledge himself to three requirements :—

(1) That he seeks the Light voluntarily, for its own sake, and from no unworthy or material motive.

(2) That his objects in seeking it are two-fold; (1) knowledge for himself, and (2) a desire to make himself, in virtue of that knowledge, of more extensive service to humanity.

(3) That he will persevere in the path about to be disclosed to him; (which means perseverance not merely through the formal Ceremony, but in pursuing throughout his subsequent daily life all that that Ceremony typifies).

It is important that these questions, too, should be answered spontaneously and without prompting. For they involve definite personal commitments of a far-reaching character to which no one should be suffered to pledge himself lightly or under persuasion.

Especially noteworthy is the second promise – that such higher knowledge as he acquires shall be used in human service. Now no one can truly serve humanity until he knows how to do so; a good deal of activity is displayed nowadays that passes by the name of service, but is not such enlightened or sanctified service as is meant by the Craft; therefore the acquisition of special knowledge is mentioned first, so that the Candidate may learn how to serve really and effectually; but, when acquired, that knowledge is not to be for selfish purposes but to be put to selfless service of the race. The enlightenment of Initiation is not to be for his private benefit only; it must become of importance to, and a trust for, the general good. Every real Initiate by the mere fact of his enlightenment, becomes so much salt and seasoning to a corrupting world; hence he is called upon not to hide his light but to use it and let it shine before men that they may see in him an example worth following.

Service, indeed, is and ever has been the ulterior motive of the Mysteries; but there are many forms of it and service can be rendered in quite other and higher ways than ordinary altruistic activity. Of these the Candidate will learn more later. But let him never forget that, at the threshold of his Masonic life, he pledged himself to become a servant of humanity

5 – The Advance from West to East

This is a small episode, yet one of far-reaching significance.

The Candidate has just completed symbolic Odyssean journeying around the Lodge, which exemplifies his benighted life wanderings since he came to birth in this world (the "West").

During his career he has passed blindly, yet never without unseen guidance, through regions and experiences sometimes of darkness (the "North"), sometimes of less or greater enlightenment (the "South," "West" and "East"), yet entirely ignorant whither he was going or what the purpose of his life was, or whether at a given moment he was near to or far from its true goal. Is not this symbolic journeying true to human life? Until one's eyes eventually are opened to the whole plan of it, who shall say whether this or that event in our personal life-experience drew us nearer to or farther from the goal we are all unwittingly seeking?

But these ignorant wanderings in a circle, these buffetings of fortune and the tests of character they constitute, at last terminate, and the moment comes when the Prodigal Son at last turns homewards and heads definitely away from the West to the East. His steps may still continue to be irregular; but no matter, they are in the right direction. Intellectually and emotionally he may still tack and wobble from side to side before he attains stable foothold and finds the straight way of peace; but where there's a will there's a way, and he who is bent on finding the way to the East at all costs will assuredly arrive there, and he will arrive bearing within his own character those certificates of fitness for higher things which are implied by the S.W. presenting the Candidate to the W.M. as a fit and proper person and properly prepared to be made a Mason.

6 – The Obligation

Following the traditional practice of the Mysteries and of all secret and monastic Orders, a vow of silence and secrecy is next required from the Candidate as a further preliminary to the conferment of Initiation and the entrustment with any secret information.

This Obligation is often thought of as merely perpetuating the usual covenant of secrecy required by new members of the old Trade Guilds as a guard to the privileges of the Guild and the protection of technical trade secrets. But whilst the Speculative Craft certainly follows the Operatives in this and other respects, the reasons for secrecy and for being solemnly obligated to it run much deeper than to the need for silence about the formal secrets of the Order.

The main purpose of the Obligation is to impress the beginner upon the path of Light and self-knowledge with a sense of the extreme value of silence about the new perceptions that will come to him, the new ideas and experiences he will encounter, and the mental reactions he will experience as the result of them. And it must be emphasized that silence and secrecy are imposed not so much in the interest of the Fraternity at large (which could suffer little from his indiscretions) as in that of the individual Brother himself. Experience will teach him, later on, the deep personal value of silence. He will find that Light and Wisdom are acquired not from anything that can be ocularly shewn or orally imparted to him, but from the gradual assembly of new ideas and their gradual digestion and co-ordination by his own mind, for which purpose it is above all things essential that his mental energies should be conserved, not frittered away in talk. To use an electrical analogy, he must become an "accumulator," receiving new impressions and letting them revolve in the closed circle of his own mind. which will gradually digest them and extract their final values.

In the world without the Lodge an appalling waste of human energy occurs daily in the form of needless private chatter and public utterance, which might be re-directed to higher ends. The way of the inner life, upon which one symbolically enters on passing the door of the Lodge, is the reverse. It calls for silence and economy of speech. It remembers one's moral accountability for each spoken word. And because it calls for the conservation of one's verbal energies and prohibits their needless diffusion in frothy exuberance, it leads by deep and still waters of knowledge, and silence generates the power needed for speaking with authority and effect when the time for such speaking comes.

Turn now to the V.S.L., the Mason's supreme light in these matters. It declares "There is a time to be silent and a time to speak," (Ecc. III., 7). Note that the time for silence comes first in orders; for indeed it is not possible to "speak" at all in the high sense here implied until, by a previous discipline of silence, one has acquired the wisdom to know what to say, how, when, and to whom to say it, and is possessed of the spiritual momentum which transforms ordinary speech into winged "words of power." Only after a long discipline of silence is it that "out of the fulness of the heart the mouth speaketh."

It is common with newly made Brethren in the first flush of their new Masonic life to find hosts of new perceptions and ideas welling up in their minds as the result of Initiation and of the thoughts and studies to which their Initiation has led them. To these they feel impelled to give expression, and to teach and share with others things they are just beginning to learn themselves. It is always satisfactory to find that the forces of Initiation have proved effective in them and have kindled their inner fire even to that extent; but it is precisely to the curbing of this crude enthusiasm, that the Obligation is largely directed at silence is ordained, and that we owe the traditional practice of restricting the giving of instruction in Masonic science to those who have become Masters of it and for whom the "time to speak" has come.

For peril attaches to premature and unwise speech no less than to more flagrant violations of secrecy; a peril pointed to in the penalty of the Obligation. That penalty (when we discern the spiritual intention behind the literal expression of it) implies that he who is unfaithful to his duly of silence and secrecy may come to lose the power of effective speech altogether. By frittering away energies which need to be conserved and consolidated he may automatically render himself spiritually unvocal. Says a wise old counsel :—

Word is thrall but Thought makes free; Hold thy speech, I counsel thee.

Observe this further point. The Candidate takes the Obligation upon the visible emblem of the ever-speaking Divine Word (than which nothing is more continually speaking yet nothing is more silent), and by a manual act attaches himself to and indents himself with it. By emulating its silence he may eventually recover that Lost Word for which Masonry is the search, and become able to sound it forth through his own person.

A word upon the posture observed during the Obligation, and compare it with what has previously been said about the partial measure of symbolical disrobing the Candidate undergoes in this Degree. Remember also the changing and progressive nature of both the posture and the measure of disrobement adopted during the three Degrees, for they are deeply significant. They imply that, before the aspirant can attain a new regenerate self, his old selfhood must become broken down, its pride humbled, its attachment to external possessions and ingrained mental prejudices severed. All which is not the work of a moment but a gradual process. He is, therefore, not called upon to do anything beyond his immediate powers, but to follow the principle of "precept upon precept; line upon line; here a little and there a little." Hence it is that the posture (and the unclothing) change in each Degree and affect different limbs and parts of the Candidate's person. In the First Degree only one knee rests on the ground; in the Second it will he the other knee that will mark his progressive humility; whilst in the Third the posture will signify that his humility is no longer partial but total, and that all resistance of mind and stubbornness of will have at last sunk to complete self-surrender to the Good Law upon whose symbolic volume he places first one hand and finally both.

7 – The Restoration to Light

The Candidate is next reminded that for a considerable time he has been in a state of darkness.

Let no one be so literally-minded as to imagine that this naïve and simple phrase alludes merely to the few minutes during which the Candidate's sight has been shut off for symbolic reasons. Remember that the whole ceremony is allegory, a parable of the soul's life; that it dramatises in small "the entry" of all men upon this their mortal existence"; and that the entirety of that existence has hitherto been spent in a state of darkness and blindness and will so continue to be spent until that spiritual consciousness is regained which we call "Light."

"Our birth is but a sleep and a forgetting," says the poet. Our re-birth, he might have added, is an awakening and a remembering; but it comes about only when there is kindled within us that latent central "Light," to seek which is the purpose of our entrance into this world and to find which is really the predominant wish of every human heart, whether that wish becomes a definite conscious urge or remains dormant and subconscious.

In every Candidate that wish is presumed to have become a definite conscious urge, and because it has become so predominant and overpowering in him that he is without peace of soul until he finds what he has been blindly seeking, he is, by the law of life itself, entitled to have his prayer answered, to have the door opened to his own knocking, and to hear spoken over him the fiat of his own re-creation, "Let there be Light."

Throughout our Ritual by "Light" we must understand "consciousness." "Let there be Light" implies, therefore, "let there be a quickening, heightening and expansion of consciousness in that which has hitherto been unconscious, or but limitedly conscious."

Some measure of consciousness is present in everything, in every kingdom of Nature, from mineral to man. In man is gathered up the consciousness of all the sub-human kingdoms, and in him that consciousness is capable of being advanced still farther; indeed, to a stage beyond the human.

Our First Degree, therefore, implies the first stage of an expansion of consciousness beyond that of the normal mentality. The Second Degree implies a still farther advancement; the Third implies a "raising" to a still higher one; whilst the Supreme Degree of the Royal Arch points to a final sublime "exaltation" of consciousness to which the prior Craft Degrees lead up.

Throughout the sequence of grades is implied a progressive advance from the normal natural mentality to the heights of spiritual consciousness, an advance which is biblically spoken of as "ascending the Hill of the Lord." And each of our Masonic ceremonies has been designed to promote a grade in that ascent.

How far that ascent will be promoted by a particular ceremony, how far a Candidate's conscience may be thereby quickened and expanded, depends upon a combination of three conditions; (1) the help of God; (2) the preparedness of the Candidate; (3) the efficiency of the Lodge and the Initiating Master as instruments for bringing the two former into union.

It need not be supposed that an actual accession of spiritual consciousness to the Candidate comes about instantly and simultaneously with the symbolic act of restoration to light. It may or may not do so. Usually new consciousness emerges but slowly through the darkness of our clouded understanding. To use Masonic analogy, the Sun at the center of our personal system only mounts to the meridian gradually; there is first a dawn and a gradual rising and a scattering of the darkness before its light manifests in fullness and strength at high noon.

Significance, of course, attaches to the symbolic "firing" in which all present engage at the moment of restoration to light. It is, as it were, a discharge or liberation of the tension to which the assembly has been subjected during the ceremony; it is the outward expression of their co-operation with the Initiating Master in bringing the Candidate from darkness to light; whilst to the Candidate himself it should mean the sound of the breaking of his inward fetters, resulting in that uplifting of soul and sudden access of vision which enables him to say "Whereas before I was blind, now I see!"

Summary of Part I

The Restoration to Light, the climax and peak-point of the Ceremony, concludes that first portion of it, that series of seven ascending steps of the mystical Mountain, which are associated with his "state of darkness." The remainder of the Ceremony, a series of seven descending steps, occurs in the newly won "state of light," and is devoted to imparting information and instruction in regard to conserving, nourishing and developing that Light within oneself, now that it has once been glimpsed.

Before passing on to this, let us summarize what has preceded. The Ceremony has dramatized in symbolic, swiftly-moving, but comprehensive ritual-form the path to be allowed by anyone who, under the stress of his own deepest heart-impulses, turns in discontent from the interests of the natural world without, in quest of those of the world within. It explains his own nature and his own past life to him; it indicates the conditions and terms upon which a re-orientation of himself and the satisfaction of his hopes are possible to him; it shows that he must empty himself of his old self, divesting and detaching himself from his past acquisitions, whether intellectual or material. These – his "personal comforts" —will, like those literal ones of the Candidate's, all be restored to him later on, but what new values will they then take on! how amplified and multiplied will their value become to him, who, like Job, has consented to be stripped of them that he may find a higher good! To which end, further, he must make a great adventure of faith; letting all go; surrendering himself to invisible guidance; maintaining a resolute will to find what he seeks; breaking down all opposition and interference between himself and his goal; and dedicating himself to the source of Light and to becoming, as a light-bearer himself, an instrument for forms of human service higher than he could ever render without it.

Such is the path of real Initiation as marked out in this Ceremony. It involves blinding the eyes, baring the heart, and tyling the mind to things external and shadowy that they may open again upon things internal and substantial in a true Restoration to Light.

Then comes the Sun's Light to our hut When fast the senses' door is shut. For such a pure and perfect guest The emptiest room is furnished best.

If the Ceremony does not mean all this, it means nothing worthy of pursuing and is but a vain tradition and formality. If it means all this, but is performed without understanding and without transplanting its implications into our life-conduct, we profane it, increase our own darkness, and act no differently from those who turn mechanical praying-wheels. But if the dispersion of our natural darkness and the rising into consciousness above it of that Sun which glows at the centre of every man's personal system be what we look for, then in our Ceremony surely we have in our hands a means of grace of the first value and efficacy.

PART II

8 – The Revelation of the Greater and the Lesser Lights

It is impossible to formulate in words the condition resulting from actual "restoration to Light." Psychological states are indescribable and must be experienced before they can be understood. But an analogy may help us to an understanding of the enlargement of consciousness which real Initiation effects; for the re-birth of one's mind and spiritual nature (which, as we have said, is implied by Initiation) stands in exact correspondence with, and follows the same law and process as physical birth; the process of "birth" is repeated upon a higher level of the spiral of creation.

Now when a child is born into this world physically, it, as it were, undergoes an initiation into a new state of existence and attains a consciousness which it never previously experienced, and it requires some considerable time before its consciousness becomes adjusted to its new environment, and its vision duly focused upon objects around it. It is only conscious vaguely and incoherently; time and practice are requisite before it can accustom itself and its eyesight to its surroundings.

Similarly with psychological rebirth. Individual experience of it varies, but broadly one passes into a state of awareness of something having happened in oneself of an expanding and illuminating character. One cannot tell oneself, let alone others, what it is; one merely knows that there has been an upheaval from within, a shifting of one's focus of consciousness from a lower to a higher level, entailing a feeling of liberation from former mental limitations, the promise of much wider mental vision and deeper understanding for the future, and withal a sense of deep, uplifting, but inexplicable happiness. Such is a very crude description of what a duly prepared and responsive Candidate is likely to experience as the result of his Initiation; possibly, but not necessarily, during the conferment of the ceremony, but at some less or greater interval after it. He is, in biblical language, one of those who having previously sat in darkness, has now suddenly seen a great light, but cannot yet say what that light is or involves, or define any detailed perceptions. All he knows is that he has "received his sight," and that whereas before he was relatively blind, he is now at last beginning to see.

Now it will be a very promising fact, if the Candidate's Initiation result is a "restoration to light" to the extent just mentioned. For it means that subsequent reflection upon his new experience will steady his quickened emotions and facilitate the adjustment of his mental sight until it is able to attain clear precise vision of certain truths, just as an infant learns to adjust its eyes to objects around it.

Then certain great primary truths of life will gradually emerge and become revealed to him. And those great primary truths are, in our Ceremony, symbolically figured forth in what we call our "Three Great but Emblematic Lights." These emblems are actually revealed to the Candidate by the Master as the first objects upon which his eyes look after being given light, and the Candidate is appropriately kept in a kneeling posture, and facing the East, whilst they are exhibited and briefly explained; for how should one contemplate primary fundamental Divine truths save in an attitude of humility and upon one's mental knees? It is very fitting, therefore, that the Three Great Lights should be the first objects of the Candidate's perception, and that they should be revealed to him whilst facing East, and whilst in a kneeling posture.

Of what, now, are these Three Great Lights the emblems? They consist, observe, of the V.S.L., the S., and the C.; the three being always displayed as if they were organically and indissociably combined; the V.S.L. lying undermost and forming the base for the other two which rest upon it. the C. being partially concealed by the S.

These three emblems we may interpret thus :——

(1) The V.S.L., although embodying the Divine Law as - revealed to the Western world, has a far wider significance. For us Masons, it is the visible emblem of the invisible Cosmic Law, through which Deity is manifested in the Universe. It virtually, therefore, represents God Himself who, as Law, underlies everything, and is the basis of all being. "Law" has many forms or modes, and we must, therefore, not limit our ideas of it to any one of them, but rather think of it as comprising them all, as physical law, intellectual law, moral law, and as unifying the dual qualities of Justice and Mercy, of Severity and Love, which characterize the Divine Nature.

So broad is the Craft's conception of the "Sacred Law" that Masons are not committed to treating the Bible as the only expression of it. Accordingly, the Holy Scriptures of any religion are permitted to be exposed in the Lodge in substitution for the Bible; the principle adopted being that a Candidate may be obligated upon the particular revelation of Cosmic Law which he recognizes as true for himself and binding upon his conscience.

Thus in many Lodges where men of non-Christian faith are admitted, alternative sets of Scriptures are kept, so that a Jew may be obligated upon the Pentateuch, a Moslem upon the Koran, an Indian upon the Vedas or Puranas, and so on.

(2) The Compasses resting upon the V.S.L. represent the Divine Spirit or Divine Principle issuing forth from Deity into manifestation, both cosmically and in the individual, and proceeding to function in accordance with the Divine Law.

(3) The Square set opposite to, but inextricably conjoined with, the Compasses, represents the sheath or vesture of cosmic Matter, in which the Divine Spirit takes form and proceeds to function.

Read in conjunction, then, the Three Great Lights reveal the Cosmic Purpose; i.e.. Spirit and Matter working in unison and according to Divine Law to realize an idea or intention latent in the Divine Mind.

What is that Divine Idea? It is that of constructing a perfect Universe, occupied by perfect beings; a Universe in which the animating Spirit and the material form shall stand in perfect balance and, being made in the Divine image and likeness, shall be a perfect expression of the Divine Thought and a fitting tabernacle for the Deity to indwell.

Masonically, we speak of Deity as the Great Architect, and of the Universe as the Cosmic Temple in process of being built in accordance with the Divine Law and Order and with the help of the Divine Compasses and Square; and it is this idea, as being the basis of Masonic doctrine and philosophy, which is, therefore, the first "secret" revealed to every Candidate and displayed to him under the guise of our Triune Great Lights; for, as a Mason, it becomes his duty to co-operate with the Great Architect in executing His plan and erecting the Great Cosmic Temple.

Having been shewn the Three Great Lights (or, as we may call them, the three great Cosmic Principles), the Candidate is now turned around from facing the East, and shown Three Lesser Lights burning in different parts of the Lodge. Now these Three Lesser Lights stand in direct correspondence with the three great ones. They are meant to indicate to the Candidate that the three great Cosmic Principles or Lights which sublie the Universe, are reproduced and present in miniature within himself. The Universe is the Macrocosm (or great image of the Divine Thought); he himself is the Microcosm (or image in small of the same Thought), and in him too reside three "lights" enabling him to co-operate with the Great Architect's plan. To him, too, have been entrusted the Compasses of the discerning Mind to direct his own personal life; the Square of bodily form which it will be his task to work into due shape and make meet as a living stone for the Cosmic Temple; whilst the Master Light of Conscience also resides imperishably within him to indicate to him the path of duty.

By the assistance of these Three Lesser Lights the Candidate is enabled (as the Lecture of the Degree will teach him) to perceive for the first time the form of the Lodge; to behold its arrangement, its furniture and jewels, to contemplate its length, breadth and height, the disposition of the Brethren around its sides, whilst its middle portion is left as empty space and illumined by the "Glory in the Centre." Translating this into personal significance, he is meant to realize that all this external-imagery is but a picture of himself, seen from within himself and no longer from without. For just as he is now within the Lodge, and able to see what was previously closed to him, so now by the help of his own inner lights he may hope to become able to enter within himself, to contemplate introspectively the spaciousness of his own soul, to observe with what graces and jewels of character he must furnish and adorn it, and to perceive his own personal faculties at the circumference and the presence of that bright Star which blazes at his own center.

To sum up; the instruction in the Great Lights is to reveal to the Candidate the basic Law and Principles of all being; whilst that in the lesser ones constitutes his first lesson in the "knowledge of himself" and teaches him that those Principles exist also within his own soul and provide him with lights sufficient to shape it into perfection and bring himself into harmony with Cosmic Law.

In the concealment of the lower points of the C. beneath the S. lies a most instructive lesson. Thereby is implied that man's immortal and powerful spirit (represented by the C.) is at present overlain and prevented from full function by the contrary tendencies of his mortal material body, represented by the S.) Now this position must become reversed. If man is to become perfected and rise to the full height and possibilities of his being, his spiritual principle must not remain subordinated to the flesh and its tendencies, but gain ascendancy over them. This the Mason is taught to achieve for himself, and in proportion as he subdues his lower nature he will liberate the powers and faculties of his immortal spirit and rise to mastership over all that is fleshly and material in himself. In the subsequent Degrees this triumph of the spirit over the body will be symbolically evidenced by the points of the C. being progressively raised above the S, first one and then the other, until the Candidate for perfection becomes at last "able to work with both those points and render the circle of his Masonic conduct complete."

9 – The Entrustment with the Secrets

Next follows the Candidate's entrustment with the "secrets" of the Degree. This, however, is preceded by an explanation to him of certain dangers which, unknown to himself, he is told he has already passed, and he is shewn the sword and the cabletow. These, of course, are but visible symbols of certain subjective spiritual perils incident to rashly embarking upon the path of spiritual experience and to the moral suicide involved in receding from that path when one's eyes have been opened to it. To the novice these perils are imperceptible, and will not become apparent until after considerable experience; meanwhile he should accept the warning as a wise counsel from those more advanced than himself.

As to the sword that is shewn him, let him reflect upon the frequent Scriptural references to the two-edged "sword of the Spirit," to its penetrating power and the way in which it is said to guard access to the central "Tree of Life." This will help him to understand the use of the sword in the Ceremony, and why, on his first entrance to the Lodge, he is made to feel its sharp point.

To the cabletow attaches very considerable significance; indeed, so important is this item of equipment that it appears in one guise (or disguise) or another in each of the three Degrees, as also in the Royal Arch. It is not expedient that its deeper meanings should be spoken about promiscuously even among Masons; like many other things in the Craft, those meanings will either disclose themselves to advancing experience or be imparted privately by a teacher to approved pupils. It may be said, however, that biblically, the cabletow is referred to in the familiar phrase "or ever the Silver Cord is loosed" (Ecc. XII., 6) and whoever understands that phrase will perceive why the "cord" is used in each of our Ceremonies.

The "secrets" (or arcane truths) imparted in this Degree are explained as consisting of certain peculiar marks or signs, intended to distinguish all Brethren of the elementary grade of Apprentice. Outwardly, in this and in subsequent Degrees also, they are expressed by step, sign, and word. These, of course, are not the full or real secrets, but only figurative emblems of them. It is what they signify that constitutes the secrets, and that significance is left for the Candidate to meditate upon and reduce into daily personal practice. Only so will he really learn them and come to understand why they are called "secrets" and why we insist upon their use. They can never be orally communicated, except in symbolic form, but must be learned by experimental practice. Just as a prosperous business man can never convey the "secret" of his success to someone who has not himself practiced it, so the secrets of Masonic progress are learned only by those who actually live them. They are clues to spiritual progress rather than confidential communications of secret information.

In being given the formal symbolic secrets the Candidate should reflect that he is receiving a first lesson in a long course of instruction of a private and occult nature; i.e., one not taught outside the Lodge, but hidden from public knowledge and intended to help him upon the path of his personal inner life.

For having but just entered upon that path, it is proper that he should now be instructed how to tread it. He has a long journey to take to reach the goal the Craft opens to him, a goal not yet visible. Hence he should absorb instruction slowly, proceed warily, understandingly, and withal humbly. He has been given a first far-off glimpse of the Light he seeks, but that Light would only confound and blind him were it revealed to him in its fullness, suddenly and abruptly. In his quest of it he should apply to himself the well-worn words of Newman's hymn, "I do not ask to see the distant scene; one step enough for me." And it is one step, and only one step at a time, that the Craft permits and teaches in each of our Degrees. Let him see that he carries into daily life all that that one step signifies, for until he has taken it in actual living he will be incapable of taking the subsequent ones. And to the Apprentice Mason seven years are allocated to taking it, though (as the Lecture states) less will suffice if he be found worthy of preferment.

Why so long a period as seven years? The answer lies in the fact that the First Degree of spiritual and Masonic life is one of purification of body and mind in preparation for the attainment of Light in all its fullness. The unpurified natural man can never reach that Light; his own inherent, impurities and darkness will always clog his mind and keep him self-hoodwinked from it. Therefore, purification is necessary and the elimination of everything in him that clouds his vision and coarsens his nature. This takes time. We know our bodies undergo change every seven years. Physiologists declare that during that period every cell and tissue of us undergoes renewal. The man who understands himself and resolutely sets about at the work of regeneration can, therefore, rely on Nature's assistance in enabling him within seven years gradually to work off his own impurities and replace them with new material, thus building a cleaner, purer body for himself, one better fitted for being suffused by the Light resident at his own center. This "septenary law" – one of the key-secrets for interpreting life – was well known to the Initiates of old and it is for this reason that seven years are allotted to the work of the First Degree.

There is much to be learned about the "word" of the Degree and the posture in which it is imparted, but this again must be left to private oral tuition. The directions about the Candidate being "expected to stand perfectly erect," and the references to "right (i.e., straight) lines and angles" and "well-squared actions" comprise a wealth of allusion to secret truths into which the average Brother never thinks it worth-while to inquire. To the experienced, however, such matters as bodily posture and the "well-squaring" of one's personal actions (even in such minute matters as writing legibly and with every letter well- formed) have both a physiological and a character value of great importance in relation to the effort to attain spiritual perfection. Nature has had a purpose in slowly raising man's animal body from a horizontal to an erect posture and in transforming his animal instincts and passions into moral rectitude, and she has still further purposes to disclose as resulting from physiological erectness. "Unto the upright ariseth light in the darkness," says the Psalmist; and to Initiates this is literally true. It is a part of their training and discipline to adopt a physically erect posture of the spinal column when engaged in their devotions and meditations, that pillar-like posture being known to be conducive to the attainment of spiritual consciousness or "light." Hence all prayers in the Lodge are said with the Brethren upstanding, for which reason the Masonic Candidate is instructed to "stand perfectly erect" at the moment when the light of the "word" is communicated to him. In former times, for well understood psycho-physiological reasons, a deformed or diseased person was never accepted as a fit and proper Candidate for Initiation.

As to the "Word" given to the Candidate, a brief hint may be given here. It is said to denote Strength; a better rendering would be Power, Energy, Ardor, all of which are implied by it. It refers to the energy and ardor with which the Candidate should pursue his work of self-perfecting now that he has once begun it; and the word is given him because keeness and energy will prove one of the key-secrets of his successful progress. All creative work depends upon two interacting active and passive forces, energy and resistance, labor and rest. (In the Creation God first labored and then rested). The Ceremony reminds us that these two forces were represented at the forefront of Solomon's symbolic temple by two "pillars," i.e., foundation principles. And it is these two principles – activity and contemplation – that the Candidate must learn to apply to himself in rebuilding his own personal temple.

10 – The Testing by the Wardens

Following the entrustment with the Secrets, the Candidate is directed to be led to each Warden in turn and told to communicate them to him. Why is this? It is to ascertain whether he retains the instructions and impressions already communicated to him and can reproduce them, or whether he will fail in so doing, or will pervert or falsify them. In a word he is subjected to a test of his own capacity to retain and live up to what has already been imparted to him.

This episode not only perpetuates the practice of the Ancient Mysteries but is entirely accordant with Scriptural authority and with spiritual experience. For it is a fact, indeed a law, of life, that no one receives an accession of knowledge or power or even of material wealth without being soon afterwards put to a test as to how he will use it and whether he is able and worthy to retain it, if he is, he will be still further advanced; not, he will remain where he was or be degraded to a worse position than at first. 'To him that hath shall be given; and from him that hath not shall be taken away even that which he hath." Remember to what a severe testing Job was subjected after acquiring great wealth; remember, too, the "temptation" or testing episode related in the Gospels as occurring to Jesus immediately after his accession of spiritual light at the Jordan baptism.

And so it will be to everyone for whom our Initiation Ceremony becomes translated into terms of actual life-experience. As soon as Light or Wisdom has been vouchsafed him, he will find himself tested in one or another way as to his worthiness to receive it. "He who has not been tested knows nothing" says a wise Master (Thomas a Kempis), for no new truth can become one's own until it has been reduced to personal conduct and lived out under the stress of opposition and temptation to the contrary.

Earlier in our Ceremony, you will remember, the Candidate was conducted to the Wardens in turn and, arousing them from silence, provoked them to speak to him; and it was explained that in doing so the Candidate was symbolically calling into activity certain higher forces latent in himself but previously dormant. It is those same latent forces or higher principles in himself that will put him to the test now that his intelligence has been accorded a certain small measure of Light. Can he retain that Light? Does he still exhibit the "sign" of a true Mason? Is he still striving to tread the path and to take the "step"? Does he remember and act upon the "word" that was given him"? Does his daily life show that he is uttering that word, – if not in its completeness, at least in broken syllables or letters? (Our practice of "half-ing" or "lettering" the word is not merely for precautionary reasons or to show that we share its secret with other Brethren, but as a most instructive and delicate reminder that though we be unable to utter that word in its entirety, yet if we can only sound it forth in stumbling but sincere fragmentary efforts, those fragments will suffice to let us pass our test).

If, therefore, we pass the test, we are permitted and directed to pass on to higher attainments, and it is of this that the sending around of the Candidate to the Wardens to prove himself a Mason is a dramatic and symbolic representation.

11 – The Investiture with the Apron

Since each episode in the Ceremony follows its predecessor with far-seeing wisdom and psychological accuracy, we shall now see how great and fitting a reward awaits the Candidate as the result of passing the test to which he has just been submitted.

On the S.W. reporting to the Master that the Candidate has made real and demonstrable progress in the science, the Master forthwith gives directions for the investment with the Apron. Thereupon, for the first time the Candidate becomes masonically clothed and entitled thenceforth to wear the glorious badge of the Order.

Behind this act of investment lies an important but ultra-physical truth, namely, that every spiritual state into which the human soul passes is accompanied by an appropriate bodily form.

The ancient maxim of the Initiates about this is "Nullus spiritus sine indumento;" no spirit (or spiritual condition) exists without possessing its appropriate form or garment; or, in Scriptural words, "God giveth it a body as it pleaseth Him, and to every seed (or soul) its own body." And accordingly, on the Candidate being certified as having attained a new phase of soul-growth, the Master (as the Divine representative in the Lodge) at once orders him to be clothed upon with a vesture expressive of his spiritual condition.

How fitting a vesture the Apron is will appear on perceiving its emblematic value. It is at once one of the most important and comprehensive of our symbols. Its shape is that of an equilateral triangle, superimposed upon a quadrangle whose sides are equal also. The triangle is the primitive and universal emblem of what is Spiritual and Formless, whilst the quadrangle is that of what is Material and possesses Form (or body); and, since human nature is a compound of both, the Apron is a figure of man himself. And because the triangle and quadrangle are among the most ancient ideographs in the world, and indeed as old as humanity itself, the Apron is very truly described as being "a badge older than that of any other Order in existence."

The Apron is also of white lambskin; an emblem, therefore, of purity, of innocence, and infancy; an appropriate clothing for one just born into the Masonic life. It is five-pointed, in allusion to man's five-sensed nature and to many other occult truths concerning humanity. If you add the three sides of its triangular part to the four of its quadrangular, you get seven, the number of completeness in Nature, corresponding with the septenary of colors in the spectrum, the notes of the musical scale, and the days of the week. If you multiply them, you get twelve, the cosmic number, comprising the twelve Zodiacal Signs through which our Solar System moves and which are reflected in the twelve Hebrew Tribes and the twelve Apostles.

As the Candidate advances through the Degrees and perhaps eventually becomes advanced to the higher sections of the Masonic Hierarchy, he will find at each new step a corresponding change in the form and colors of his Apron. It will manifest what are known as the sacred or royal colors, blue, purple and scarlet, whilst to its unadorned simplicity will be added ornamentations of the precious metals, at first silver and afterwards gold. These elaborations of the Apron are meant to symbolize corresponding progress in him who wears it, and point to the unfolding of spiritual graces and powers from the depths of his own inward being. As the strength of his central spirit grows, so his Apron will burgeon forth in symbolic rosettes and become decorated with celestial blue and ornaments of silver; and, as it intensifies still further, the pale azure will deepen correspondingly to royal blue, and silver will be displaced by gold, – the emblem of wisdom and spiritual royalty. The Apron, moreover, is attached to the body by a fastener in the form of a serpent – the emblem of Wisdom, to indicate the wisdom with which his whole organism has been devised.

Let the Candidate, then, see in the Apron a symbol of himself and, in its progressive beautifying, reflect that it calls for the manifestation of corresponding growth of spirituality in his own life. Let him regard his Apron with a respect comparable to that with which he should regard his own soul, keeping it so far as may be sacred and undented, never treating it with levity nor entrusting it to any hands but his own. For, being the symbol of himself, it should be respected as the outward and visible image of his inward invisible self.

As it is written that no man may enter heaven without wearing a "wedding garment" (i.e., a vesture qualifying him for union with the celestial life), so no Mason may enter a Lodge without wearing the Apron that proclaims his fellowship and amity with the universal Craft. But we need not restrict our thought or even our use of the Apron to wearing it in Lodge; it is helpful to imagine ourselves as clothed with it at all times, whether we are actually wearing it or not. There are some Brethren who gird on their Masonic clothing in private, ere engaging in their personal devotions. And there are some who, loyal to its meaning in their lifetime, like still to wear their Apron in the grave.

12 – The Charge in the N.E. Corner

Clothed upon Masonically, the Candidate is then placed in the N.E. corner of the Lodge. By "the Lodge" was formerly meant not the room in which the Ceremony takes place, but the Lodge-board or Trestle-board, now called the Tracing-board, to the N.E. corner of which the Candidate's feet were angulated; a practice still obtaining in some Lodges and one that seems desirable to pursue.

The N.E. corner is a point of much symbolic significance. It is the meeting place of N. and E., of darkness and light, and, therefore, representative of the Candidate's own condition. Standing at this point, he can henceforward at will step onward to the E., or backward to the N., advancing further to the Light or relapsing into darkness; it will rest with himself which direction his life will henceforth take.

He is charged, however, to make his present position the basis of renewed spiritual activity and to regard his personality as a "foundation-stone," now well and truly laid, as the material for raising thereon a "super-structure." By this expression is meant something much more than mere character-building, as it is often thought to mean. What is implied may perhaps be gathered by reference to some of the older Masonic rituals in which a "castle in the air," an expression which, far from meaning something dreamy and imaginary as it popularly has come to do, really refers to an "airy," ethereal or spiritual body, "a house not made with hands nor subject to decay (like his temporal body) but eternal and heavenly."

This leads one into deeper metaphysics than can be dealt with here, and the subject must be left to private reflection and tuition, with merely the hint that as our mortal visible body has been built up gradually, cell by cell and tissue by tissue, out of the essences and life forces of temporal Nature, so Man has within him the capacity to raise thereupon, and to evolve from himself, an immortal invisible "super-structure." an "airy" castle or fortress into which his conscious soul will retreat and clothe itself when its earthly vesture fall away. The erection of the super-structure is known in Masonic mysticism as the "building King Solomon's Temple," which every Mason must build for himself.

A further subject upon which the Candidate is charged in the N.E. corner is the duty of Charity, the complete attainment of which is elsewhere spoken of as the summit of the Mason's profession. Now it is idle to think of this virtue and its attainment as being fulfilled by money-donations to those who are financially poor, distressed or deserving. The usual words of the Ritual may suggest that it does, but remember that the Ritual throughout is a veil, and always masks far deeper truths than its surface-words exhibit.

The "Charity" the Candidate is so earnestly entreated to cultivate at this important moment and throughout his subsequent life would perhaps be best interpreted by the word "compassion," – universal compassion for, and sympathetic feeling with, all living creatures, human and sub-human. Such a definition includes Love, which is the usual synonym for Charity, but it embraces even something more. "Charity," in its Latin original *Caritas*, means "dearness," and the Masonic virtue and duty is that of regarding all creatures in a spirit of universal and impartial dearness, as being all pilgrims upon a single path and, whilst in differing degrees of development, yet all evolving towards a common goal. In their struggles and sufferings to work out that destiny, which is theirs no less than yours, and whether they are conscious of that destiny or not, and whether they will thank you for your help or not, it is nevertheless the Mason's duty to give them all the compassion and help he can.

Giving what is personal and material is the lowest and not always a wise, form of giving. Giving mental and moral succor is relief of far greater value, because it braces the mental and moral nature of the recipients. Giving oneself from the heart in a constant sacrificial outpouring of the spirit may yield no visible result but is yet the highest of all forms of giving, and it is this which the Mason is counselled to practice, since what he radiates will quicken the life of all around him and send forth leaves from his own tree of life for the healing of the nations. At the Centre of each man's personal system dwells a sun, clouded though it may now be by the fogs and mists of his own making, which, like the solar orb in Nature, can send forth its generous beneficent radiation persistently, unstintingly, and impartially to the good and the evil alike. All the great teachers and enlighteners of humanity have been suns in that sense and because their lives were based upon compassion for the whole world; and it is for the Initiate to try to emulate them.

Consider the philosophy of giving and why it must needs be more blessed than receiving. Natural man is necessarily selfish, grasping, self-acquisitive. All his days he has been receiving – from Nature, from his parents, from society – and has become egocentric and habituated and trained to securing for himself a living, a position, and an individuality. But the Mason is a man who, by the very fact of his seeking Initiation, is impelled by forces within himself to rise beyond Nature and to submit himself to a law higher than that of self-acquisition. All his energies have now to be reversed; getting must give way to giving; centripetal tendencies must become transformed to centrifugal radiation of the highest qualities in him. In Matthew Arnold's words :—

Know, man is all that Nature is but more,

And in that "more" lie all his hopes of good. From that "more" the Mason builds a "super- structure" upon the foundation of his old self; not as formerly, by a process of getting and receiving but by one of giving forth that others may live. And the more he gives the more he must eventually receive, for all energy is conserved and, like expanding water-ripples, returns upon its source, enriched by every contact it has made in its passage.

Hence it is that the Candidate is charged to learn that self-giving is the foundation-law and foundation-stone of the higher life; that Charity has its degrees and may be practiced in many ways and upon different planes, the highest of which is the habitual pouring forth of compassionate love to all beings; that he who has freely received must as freely give; and that as he, by his Initiation, has been given the blessing of light and understanding he never before possessed, so now the Law of life itself requires that, from this moment, he shall never withhold that light from any who asks it from him.

Surely one of the most moving moments of an impressive Ceremony is that in which the Candidate, pauperized and denuded of everything material, is invited to make a gift to his poor and distressed fellow-creatures. Out of what resources can he make it save from treasury of his own heart – without the backing of which no gift, whatever its form, can have any true value? The incident is meant to teach him that if that treasury be empty how can he really give at all, however opulent he be pecuniarily? but if it be filled, he will be giving what guineas cannot buy.

13 – The Working Tools

In the N.E. Corner the Candidate is advised what to do, what to aim at, in order to promote his own advancement. The next thing is to tell him how to do it. He is, therefore, recommended to pursue certain lines of self-discipline and self-improvement which are referred to under the guise of "working tools."

These working tools are three, and as their mystical significance is sufficiently explained on their presentation to the Candidate it is needless to repeat it here. They must not be looked upon, however, as merely emblems incidental to the Ceremony and thereafter to be ignored or forgotten, but as representing duties essential to Masonic progress and meant to be put to practical daily observance.

One of these three tools, the measuring gauge, is itself threefold in its application. It allocates one's daily time to the performance of three distinct duties, duties not necessarily involving equal expenditure of time, but duties each of which is of equal value.

It inculcates (1) a duty to God and a persistent devotion to spiritual things, (2) a duty to oneself, involving due attention to material pursuits and the care of one's own person, and altruistic duty to those less happily placed than oneself; as it were an equilateral triangle of duties each of which is as important as the other two, indeed it will be helpful to think of the sides of such a triangle as signifying God, oneself, and one's neighbor respectively, and constituting a unity, a whole of which each part is necessary to the others.

The Mason must find a way of balancing his performance of these three duties, so as to make of them an equilateral and not an unequally-sided triangle. Equal attention is called for to spiritual things, to himself, and to what is other than himself, i.e., his neighbor; undue preponderance in either direction will prevent a true balance. That is why, whilst told to give altruistic help to his neighbor, he is also told that he should not do so "unless he can do it without detriment to himself or connections." At first blush these qualifying words sound selfish, contrary to the spirit, if self-sacrifice. But there is great wisdom in them. For only he can really serve and help another who has first discharged his duty to himself and made himself competent to serve. "Self-love (says Shakespeare) is not so vile a sin as self-neglect"; and there are many people who neglect to improve themselves, whilst fussily trying to improve others. But selfishness will itself disappear if devotion be habitually accorded to what is higher than self, and this attainment will then in turn qualify him to help his neighbor.

As the Candidate progresses he will learn of other working tools in the further Degrees, but these he will find himself unable to use unless he has first accustomed himself to those of the First Degree. Therefore, he is counselled to slur nothing over, but to pay attention to even the minutest instructions of the Ritual until they suffuse his life and their performance becomes a habit. He will find his education greatly helped if he will enter upon the systematic reading of literature dealing with Masonic and cognate subjects. "Reading is good prayer" says an old counsel, provided it be of a kind that helps one's quest for Light, and since Masonry is so largely a work of the mind, every study that conduces to the expansion of his mental faculties will prove a "working tool" and open fresh doors of perception to him,

14 – The Tracing Board

The concluding instruction to the Candidate is the explanation of the Tracing Board, though for convenience this is often deferred to another occasion, since it is necessarily lengthy.

It will have been observed that the Candidate has already been instructed in certain spiritual and ethical matters; and there now only remains to supplement these by appealing to his intellectual nature. This is done by introducing him to the Tracing Board and imparting to him certain esoteric information of a philosophical character. By "esoteric" is meant information not imparted outside the Lodge or taught by churches and other systems provided for public instruction, but which has always been reserved for more private and advanced tuition and which has been perpetuated in secret and embodied in hieroglyphic or symbolic pictures. At one time these cryptic designs were never exposed to the risk of public gaze. but were drawn upon the floor of the Lodge by the Initiating Master when occasion required and were expunged by the Candidate at the close of the Ceremony. Today they are kept permanently depicted upon the Lodge Board. A detailed examination of the First Degree Tracing Board appears in a previous Lodge Paper, and need not, therefore, be repeated here.

In the official Lecture explaining the Board the new Mason is recommended "to seek a Master and from him gain instruction," once more instancing the truth "Seek and ye shall find." This refers to an age-old practice by which every junior

Brother sought out and attached himself for seven years to an expert Master for the purpose of gaining much fuller private tuition in the science than is possible at meetings of the Lodge. The relationship of Master and Apprentice, which obtained in the Trade Guilds and later on became an ordinary business practice, was originally one in which the Master undertook not the commercial but the spiritual training of the neotype, a practice which obtains throughout the East to-day and which was always observed in the Mysteries of antiquity. With us the practice has, unfortunately, fallen into desuetude because so few Masters are competent to teach and so few Candidates are wishful or even ripe to learn what lies beneath the surface of the Craft doctrine.

Where, however, the true relationship of Master and Disciple does exist it becomes an intimate and precious one, involving the forging of a spiritual tie and a reciprocal responsibility which neither of them would lightly sever. This is a subject about which far more can be said than is possible here, but let us reflect that old maxim of our science is that "when the pupil is ready the Master will be found waiting," and that such Master will impart personal instruction of a far deeper and wider character than can be given publicly or promiscuously.

Finally, the Candidate is told to retire from the Lodge to be restored to what are called, a little ironically, his "personal comforts" – the poor trappings and belongings he surrendered before entering a place where such possessions have no value. Nevertheless, a pointed lesson lies in his being directed to resume them, for henceforth it will be his duty to recast his estimate of them, and. whilst using them for what they are worth, to learn to discriminate between what is of transient and what is of enduring moment. What he has hitherto deemed and clung to as "comforts" he may find to be irksome discomforts later on, until he acquires that wisdom and balanced understanding which reacts neither to comfort nor discomfort, but looks beyond both.

* * * * *

The "Ancient Charge" with which the Ceremony usually concludes is self-explanatory and need not be examined here. Strictly it is not an integral factor of the Ceremony, from which it differs both in method and language. The Ceremony proper is "veiled in allegory" and contains cryptic phrases and subsurface allusions at every turn, whilst the "Ancient Charge" has no ulterior meaning whatever. It is merely a simple homily complimenting the Candidate upon his reception into the Order and informing him of some observances with which he will be expected to comply.

The Charge obviously embodies advice formerly tendered to young men on becoming apprenticed to the Operative Building Guilds, enjoining them to good citizenship and to leading a moral and useful life. But as present-day Candidates for Speculative Masonry are assumed to hold these qualifications before joining the Craft, the Charge is of interest only as perpetuating an old custom of the Trade Guilds on admitting an Apprentice to membership.

Conclusion

Summing up this examination of the Ceremony, then, we see its purpose is as follows. The first half of it designed to restore to Light (in the spiritual sense already explained) a Candidate who seeks Light from his heart and comes prepared in mind and person to receive it. The second and complementary half of it is meant to teach him who has been brought to that Light, how to retain it and increase it, so that he may never relapse into his former darkness.

In being initiated a Candidate is being vouchsafed an initial glimpse into supra-natural Light, but only a first glimpse; it rests with himself to prove worthy of it and to enlarge that temporary glimpse into wider and permanent vision. The Ceremony dramatizes, in a few swift episodes and pregnant words, the "Apprentice" stage of the spiritual life; it inculcates that, with increasing self-purification and discipline of his material nature, the light of that spiritual Sun which burns and blazes at his own center and which has now for the first time appeared above his conscious horizon, will manifest in ever-increasing power. As that Sun rises higher and higher within him, so will his own darkness become correspondingly dispelled, and his materialism spiritualized, and his personality transformed into a translucent vessel. "If thine eye (soul) be single (simple and unadulterated by passion and wrong notions), thy whole being will be full of Light."

He is taught by that Light to see that the substratum of all things is Divine Law, Law which comprises physical, moral, and ultra-physical aspects, and in which the roots of his own being are integrated; and, therefore, in proportion as he unifies his personal will with the Universal Will and harmonizes his mind and conduct with their Cosmic Prototype, he must needs become a more perfect expression of them and a conscious collaborator with them. And because Love is the fulfilling of the Law, he is enjoined to cultivate that boundless charity and compassion towards all beings which bears, believes, hopes and endures all things, because it under stands the operation of that Law and sees clearly the end to which it is shaping us. *Tout aimer, c'est tout comprendre.*

The Apprentice stage of Masonry is, therefore, one of purification, education and self- control, which every Brother must work out and live out for himself. No amount of book knowledge or instruction from others can teach him what can be learned only from his own experience and effort. Even these notes, lengthy as they are, are but an elementary preface to far deeper aspects of Initiation than can be spoken of openly, yet which any ardent aspirant may come to learn as he proceeds. To tell the fuller truths about the subject would scare and discourage rather than enlighten and help; and for this reason the science is and always was a veiled and secret one.

One useful counsel may be added which the Candidate should observe if he wishes to progress. It is, never to measure what he finds within the Lodge by his own opinions or by the same standard of judgment that he applies to things without it. Many Brethren go wrong here by lacking humility and teachableness. They try to look at matters of the inner life with the same eyes as those of the outer life. They reserve their ideas of Masonry till they see how far they can square it with other views and beliefs that they hold, and they seek to apply their worldly wisdom to a wisdom which is hidden and not of this world, and their "common sense" to a subject requiring a special education and the use of a sense which in the present state of human evolution is far from common. But spiritual things must be spiritually discerned and not from the standpoint of unenlightened opinion and unspiritual perception.

He who enters the Lodge in quest of Light should leave all his previous learning behind him with his garments and loose the shoes of personal opinion from off his feet. He should think of himself as a child, and as being taken into a world of new sights and sounds, and where new ideas and even a different logic obtain from those with which he has previously been familiar, and where he must begin to recast his ideas and his life. Will his pride suffer him to stultify himself to this extent?

If it will not, he will but continue to darken his own light and the Craft can teach him nothing of value whatever titular rank he may attain in it. If it will, then he may hope to become an Initiate intact, as well as in name and to find his eyes opening to depth beyond depth of truth of which he is at present unconscious.

In the Mysteries of old the Candidate, because of his new birth into Light, was always spoken of as a "child" or a "little child," and in the Sacred Volume which forms the chief textbook of our science we find how often, and for the same reason, such expressions as "the young man" and "little children" are employed.

It accords little with the modern mental temper to cast aside all one's knowledge and preconceptions and reduce oneself to the docility, the naivete and singlemindedness of infancy. Yet these qualities still remain indispensable to the Candidate for Wisdom, and it still is not the learned, the critical, and the wordly-wise, but the "little children" who are suffered to come to the Light and are not forbidden from finding it, for of such are both the Kingdom of Heaven and the Craft of Masonry which is designed to lead to that Kingdom.

A Note upon the Frontispiece

The picture forming the Frontispiece to these pages not only depicts the Sign of Silence, but is a symbolic illustration of one who has attained complete Initiation and Illumination.

The beautified arched design framing the figure is know as the Vesica Piscis. "This mysterious figure (says Dr. Oliver, the well-known Masonic authority) possessed an unabounded influence on the details of sacred architecture, and constituted the great and enduring secret of our ancient brethren." It formed the geometrical basis of the great Christian cathedrals, and was the womb-shaped symbol of Initiation and of Candidates being thereby brought to spiritual re-birth.

The aureole or solar imbus around the head typifies the Candidate's attainment of spiritual consciousness; the "Sun" at the center of his personal system has fully risen above his mental horizon and illuminated his mind.

His clothing, a white inner tunic surmounted by a black cloak, typifies the separation of light and darkness in himself. The darkness of his outward mind and nature is dispelled by the light and purity of the soul within. This is the result of his following the secret path of Initiation in regard to which the Sign of Silence or Sign of the Child attaches.